About this Learning Guide

Shmoop Will Make You a Better Lover*
*of Literature, History, Poetry, Life...

Our lively learning guides are written by experts and educators who want to show your brain a good time. Shmoop writers come primarily from Ph.D. programs at top universities, including Stanford, Harvard, and UC Berkeley.

Want more Shmoop? We cover literature, poetry, bestsellers, music, US history, civics, biographies (and the list keeps growing). Drop by our website to see the latest.

www.shmoop.com

Table of Contents

Introduction

In a Nutshell

Robert Browning published "My Last Duchess" in 1842 in a book of poems titled *Dramatic Lyrics*. As the title suggests, in these poems Browning experiments with form, combining some aspects of stage plays and some aspects of Romantic verse to create a new type of poetry for his own Victorian age. The Victorians are the poor unfortunates who come between the Romantics and the Modernists. In other words, authors in this period got sandwiched between two great movements that majorly influenced Western Culture, and so readers sometimes forget about the Victorian age writers.

It's important to notice that "My Last Duchess" is one of the poems that falls into this somewhat problematic in-between age. (For reference, you can think of the Victorian era as stretching from 1837-1901. At least, those are the years when Victoria was Queen of England. Keep in mind that literary movements only correspond roughly with her reign.)

For the most part, poetry didn't do so well in the Victorian period – it was the age of the novel, and everyone was reading Charles Dickens, George Eliot, or "penny dreadfuls," which were the Victorian version of the sensationalist paperbacks sold in your local grocery store today. Most Victorian poets were highly experimental and, with the exception of Alfred, Lord Tennyson, not so highly popular; people kept reading the now-classic Romantic poets, like William Wordsworth and Lord Byron, instead of tuning in to the new developments in poetry.

Robert Browning alarmed his Victorian readers with psychological – and sometimes psychopathic – realism, wild formal experiments, and harsh-sounding language. These qualities, however, are what make poems like "My Last Duchess" so attractive to today's readers, who value the raw power of Browning's writing more than some of the feel-good flowery Romantic poems.

Browning's inspiration for "My Last Duchess" was the history of a Renaissance duke, Alfonso II of Ferrara, whose young wife Lucrezia died in suspicious circumstances in 1561. Lucrezia was a Medici – part of a family that was becoming one of the most powerful and wealthy in Europe at the time. During Lucrezia's lifetime, however, the Medici were just beginning to build their power base and were still considered upstarts by the other nobility. Lucrezia herself never got to enjoy riches and status; she was married at 14 and dead by 17. After her death, Alfonso courted (and eventually married) the niece of the Count of Tyrol.

Robert Browning takes this brief anecdote out of the history books and turns it into an opportunity for readers to peek inside the head of a psychopath. Although Browning hints at the real-life Renaissance back-story by putting the word "Ferrara" under the title of the poem as an epigraph, he removes the situation from most of its historical details. It's important to notice that the Duke, his previous wife, and the woman he's courting aren't named in the poem at all. Even though there were historical events that inspired the poem, the text itself has a more generalized, universal, nameless feel.

Why Should I Care?

We can understand why you might have trouble caring about "My Last Duchess" at first. After all, it's a fictional speech by a Renaissance duke who's conducting a marriage negotiation. But the themes in play here are way more interesting than the basic setup. Jealousy, sadism, murder, manipulation, a sinister atmosphere, and the inner thoughts of a psychopath – it's practically _The Silence of the Lambs_ in poem form.

If the macabre sensationalism isn't enough to draw you in, consider this: the Duke's overreaction to the Duchess's genial nature pretty much makes him a textbook example of a controlling, abusive husband who demands absolute subservience from his wife. The only difference is that he's crazy enough to think that even ordering her not to be nice to people is beneath him. In his mind, killing her is the only way to deal with the fact that she smiled at the sunset. And that reminds us of another movie from the early 90s – _Sleeping With the Enemy_.

So you can visualize the Duchess as Jodie Foster or as Julia Roberts, if you like. But the point is that this poem has several different attractions: a "true crime" feel (the real-life Duchess of Ferrara did die under suspicious circumstances) and a chilling depiction of the psychology of a man obsessed with power. If you ever wondered what was going through the head of someone on the edge, Browning's poetry is for you.

The Poem

My Last Duchess
Ferrara

THAT'S my last Duchess painted on the wall,
Looking as if she were alive. I call
That piece a wonder, now: Frà Pandolf's hands
Worked busily a day, and there she stands.
Will't please you sit and look at her? I said
"Frà Pandolf" by design, for never read
Strangers like you that pictured countenance,
The depth and passion of its earnest glance,
But to myself they turned (since none puts by
The curtain I have drawn for you, but I)
And seemed as they would ask me, if they durst,
How such a glance came there; so, not the first
Are you to turn and ask thus. Sir, 'twas not
Her husband's presence only, called that spot
Of joy into the Duchess' cheek: perhaps
Frà Pandolf chanced to say, "Her mantle laps
Over my lady's wrist too much," or "Paint
Must never hope to reproduce the faint

Half-flush that dies along her throat": such stuff
Was courtesy, she thought, and cause enough
For calling up that spot of joy. She had
A heart – how shall I say? – too soon made glad.
Too easily impressed: she liked whate'er
She looked on, and her looks went everywhere.
Sir, 'twas all one! My favor at her breast,
The dropping of the daylight in the West,
The bough of cherries some officious fool
Broke in the orchard for her, the white mule
She rode with round the terrace – all and each
Would draw from her alike the approving speech,
Or blush, at least. She thanked men, – good! but thanked
Somehow – I know not how – as if she ranked
My gift of a nine-hundred-years-old name
With anybody's gift. Who'd stoop to blame
This sort of trifling? Even had you skill
In speech – (which I have not) – to make your will
Quite clear to such an one, and say, "Just this
Or that in you disgusts me; here you miss,
Or there exceed the mark" – and if she let
Herself be lessoned so, nor plainly set
Her wits to yours, forsooth, and made excuse,
– E'en then would be some stooping; and I choose
Never to stoop. Oh sir, she smiled, no doubt,
Whene'er I passed her; but who passed without
Much the same smile? This grew; I gave commands
Then all smiles stopped together. There she stands
As if alive. Will't please you rise? We'll meet
The company below, then. I repeat,
The Count your master's known munificence
Is ample warrant that no just pretence
Of mine for dowry will be disallowed;
Though his fair daughter's self, as I avowed
At starting, is my object. Nay, we'll go
Together down, sir. Notice Neptune, though,
Taming a sea-horse, thought a rarity,
Which Claus of Innsbruck cast in bronze for me!

Overview and Line-by-Line Summary

Brief Summary

The Duke of Ferrara is negotiating with a servant for the hand of a count's daughter in marriage. (We don't know anything about the Count except that he *is* a count. And that he's

not the Count from *Sesame Street* – different guy.) During the negotiations, the Duke takes the servant upstairs into his private art gallery and shows him several of the objects in his collection.

The first of these objects is a portrait of his "last" or former duchess, painted directly on one of the walls of the gallery by a friar named Pandolf. The Duke keeps this portrait behind a curtain that only he is allowed to draw. While the servant sits on a bench looking at the portrait, the Duke describes the circumstances in which it was painted and the fate of his unfortunate former wife.

Apparently the Duchess was easily pleased: she smiled at everything, and seemed just as happy when someone brought her a branch of cherries as she did when the Duke decided to marry her. She also blushed easily. The Duchess's genial nature was enough to throw the Duke into a jealous, psychopathic rage, and he "gave commands" (45) that meant "all smiles stopped together" (46). We're guessing this means he had her killed although it's possible that he had her shut up somewhere, such as in a convent. But it's way more exciting if you interpret it as murder, and most critics do.

After telling this story to the servant of the family that might provide his next victim – er, sorry, bride – the Duke takes him back downstairs to continue their business. On the way out, the Duke points out one more of his favorite art objects: a bronze statue of Neptune taming a seahorse.

Section I (Lines 1-13)

Lines 1-2
THAT'S my last Duchess painted on the wall,
Looking as if she were alive.

- The speaker points out a lifelike portrait of his "last Duchess" that's painted on the wall.
- This tells us that the speaker is a Duke, that his wife is dead, and that someone is listening to him describe his late wife's portrait, possibly in his private art gallery.
- It also makes us wonder what makes her his "last" Duchess – for more thoughts on that phrase, check out our comments in the "What's Up With the Title?" section.

Lines 2-4
I call
That piece a wonder, now: Frà Pandolf's hands
Worked busily a day, and there she stands.

- The Duke tells his mysterious listener that the painting of the Duchess is impressively accurate.
- The painter, Frà (or "Friar") Pandolf, worked hard to achieve a realistic effect.
- Notice that the Duke's comment "there she stands" suggests that this is a full-length

portrait of the Duchess showing her entire body, not just a close-up of her face.

Line 5

Will't please you sit and look at her?

- The Duke asks his listener politely to sit down and examine the painting.
- But the politeness is somewhat fake, and the question seems more like a command. Could the listener refuse to sit down and look and listen? We don't think so.

Lines 5-13

I said
"Frà Pandolf" by design, for never read
Strangers like you that pictured countenance,
The depth and passion of its earnest glance,
But to myself they turned (since none puts by
The curtain I have drawn for you, but I)
And seemed as they would ask me, if they durst,
How such a glance came there; so, not the first
Are you to turn and ask thus.

- The Duke explains to the listener why he brought up the painter, Frà Pandolf.
- He says that he mentioned Pandolf on purpose, or "by design" (6) because strangers never examine the Duchess's portrait without looking like they want to ask the Duke how the painter put so much "depth and passion" (8) into the expression on the Duchess's face, or "countenance" (7).
- They don't actually ask, because they don't dare, but the Duke thinks he can tell that they want to.
- Parenthetically, the Duke mentions that he's always the one there to answer this question because nobody else is allowed to draw back the curtain that hangs over the portrait.
- Only the Duke is allowed to look at it or show it to anyone else. This is clearly his private gallery, and we're a little afraid of what might happen to someone who broke the rules there.

Lines 13-15

Sir, 'twas not
Her husband's presence only, called that spot
Of joy into the Duchess' cheek:
Addressing his still-unknown listener as "sir," the Duke goes into more detail about the expression on the Duchess's face in the painting.
- He describes her cheek as having a "spot / Of joy" (14-15) in it, perhaps a slight blush of pleasure.

- It wasn't just "her husband's presence" (14) that made her blush in this way, although the Duke seems to believe that it *should* have been the only thing that would.
- The Duke doesn't like the idea that anyone else might compliment his wife or do something sweet that would make her blush.

Section II (Lines 14-24)

Lines 15-21

perhaps
Frà Pandolf chanced to say, "Her mantle laps
Over my lady's wrist too much," or "Paint
Must never hope to reproduce the faint
Half-flush that dies along her throat": such stuff
Was courtesy, she thought, and cause enough
For calling up that spot of joy.

- The Duke imagines some of the ways that Frà Pandolf might have caused the Duchess to get that "spot of joy" in her face.
- He might have told her that her "mantle" (her shawl) covered her wrist too much, which is the Renaissance equivalent of saying, "man, that skirt's way too long – maybe you should hike it up a little."
- Or he might have complimented her on the becoming way that she flushes, telling her that "paint / Must never hope to reproduce" (17-18) the beautiful effect of her skin and coloring.
- The Duke thinks the Duchess would have thought that comments like this, the normal flirtatious "courtesy" (20) that noblemen would pay to noblewomen, were "cause enough" (20) to blush.
- Strangely, the Duke seems to believe that blushing in response to someone like Frà Pandolf was a decision, not an involuntary physical reaction. Notice that the Duke also seems to infuse his comments with a judgmental tone.

Lines 21-24

She had
A heart – how shall I say? – too soon made glad.
Too easily impressed: she liked whate'er
She looked on, and her looks went everywhere.

- The Duke describes the Duchess as "too soon made glad" (22) and "too easily impressed" (23). This is his main problem with her: too many things make her happy.
- Another way of looking at it is that she's not serious enough. She doesn't save her "spot of joy" for him alone. She's not the discriminating snob that he wants her to be.
- She likes everything she sees, and she sees everything.

Section III (Lines 25-35)

Lines 25-31

Sir, 'twas all one! My favor at her breast,
The dropping of the daylight in the West,
The bough of cherries some officious fool
Broke in the orchard for her, the white mule
She rode with round the terrace – all and each
Would draw from her alike the approving speech,
Or blush, at least.

- The Duke elaborates further on the Duchess's tendency to see every pleasant thing as pretty much the same.
- If he gives her a "favor" or mark of his esteem that she can wear, such as a corsage or piece of jewelry, she thanks him for it in the same way that she approves of a pretty sunset, a branch of cherries, or her white mule.
- At first the Duke suggests that she speaks of all these things equally, but then he changes his claim and admits that sometimes she doesn't say anything and just blushes in that special way.
- And maybe she's a little promiscuous – either in reality, or (more likely) in the Duke's imagination.
- Part of the problem is not just that she likes boughs of cherries – it's that some "officious fool" (27) brings them to her.
- (An "officious" person is someone who pokes their nose in and starts doing things when they're not wanted – somebody self-important who thinks they're the best person to do something, even when everyone else wishes they would just butt out.)

Lines 31-34

She thanked men, – good! but thanked
Somehow – I know not how – as if she ranked
My gift of a nine-hundred-years-old name
With anybody's gift.

- The Duke claims that, although it's all well and good to thank people for doing things for you, the way the Duchess thanked people seemed to imply that she thought the little favors they did her were just as important as what the Duke himself did for her.
- After all, the Duke gave her his "nine-hundred-years-old name" (33) – a connection to a longstanding aristocratic family with power and prestige.
- The Duke's family has been around for nearly a thousand years running things in Ferrara, and he thinks this makes him superior to the Duchess, who doesn't have the same heritage.

- He thinks the Duchess ought to value the social elevation of her marriage over the simple pleasures of life.

Lines 34-35

Who'd stoop to blame
This sort of trifling?

- The Duke asks his listener a rhetorical question: who would actually lower himself and bother to have an argument with the Duchess about her indiscriminate behavior?
- He thinks the answer is "nobody."
- We don't think that there is much open and honest communication in this relationship!

Section IV (Lines 35-47)

Lines 35-43

Even had you skill
In speech – (which I have not) – to make your will
Quite clear to such an one, and say, "Just this
Or that in you disgusts me; here you miss,
Or there exceed the mark" – and if she let
Herself be lessoned so, nor plainly set
Her wits to yours, forsooth, and made excuse,
– E'en then would be some stooping; and I choose
Never to stoop.

The Duke lists all the obstacles that prevented him from talking to the Duchess directly about his problems with her behavior.

- He claims that he doesn't have the "skill / In speech" (35-36) to explain what he wants from her – but his skillful rhetoric in the rest of the poem suggests otherwise.
- He also suggests that she might have resisted being "lessoned" (40), that is, taught a lesson by him, if she had "made excuse" (41) for her behavior instead.
- But even if he were a skilled speaker, and even if she didn't argue, he says he still wouldn't talk to her about it.
- Why? Because he thinks that bringing it up at all would be "stooping" to her level, and he refuses to do that.

Lines 43-45

Oh sir, she smiled, no doubt,
Whene'er I passed her; but who passed without
Much the same smile?

- The Duke admits to his listener (who is this guy, anyway?) that the Duchess was sweet to him – she did smile at him whenever he passed by her.
- But, he says, it's not like that was special. She smiles at everyone in the same way.

Lines 45-46

This grew; I gave commands;
Then all smiles stopped together.

- The Duke claims that "This grew" (45) – that is, the Duchess's indiscriminate kindness and appreciation of everything got more extreme.
- The Duke then "gave commands" (45) and as a result "All smiles stopped together" (46).
- Our best guess is that he had her killed, but the poem is ambiguous on this point.
- It's possible that he had her shut up in a dungeon or a nunnery, and that she's as good as dead.
- She's not his Duchess anymore – she's his "last Duchess" – so she's clearly not on the scene anymore.

Lines 46-47

There she stands
As if alive. Will't please you rise?

- The Duke ends his story of the Duchess and her painting by gesturing toward the full-body portrait again, in which she stands "As if alive" (47).

Section V (Lines 47-56)

Lines 47-48

We'll meet
The company below, then.

- The Duke invites his listener to get up and go back downstairs to the rest of the "company."
- As in line 5, this sounds like a polite invitation – but we can't imagine anyone refusing.

Lines 48-53

I repeat,
The Count your master's known munificence

Is ample warrant that no just pretence
Of mine for dowry will be disallowed;
Though his fair daughter's self, as I avowed
At starting, is my object.

- We finally learn why the Duke is talking to this guy: his listener is the servant of a Count, and the Duke is wooing the Count's daughter.
- The Duke tells the servant that he knows about the Count's wealth and generosity, or "munificence" (49), so he expects to get any reasonable dowry he asks for.
- But his main "object" (53) in the negotiations is the daughter herself, not more money.

Lines 53-54

Nay, we'll go
Together down, sir.

- The Duke's listener seems to try to get away from him (we would try, too).
- The Duke stops him and insists that they stay together as they go back to meet everyone else downstairs.

Lines 54-56

Notice Neptune, though,
Taming a sea-horse, thought a rarity,
Which Claus of Innsbruck cast in bronze for me!

- Before the Duke and his listener leave the gallery, the Duke points out one more of his art objects – a bronze statue of Neptune, the god of the sea, taming a sea-horse.
- The Duke mentions the name of the artist who cast this statue, Claus of Innsbruck, who made it specifically for him.

Technique

Symbols, Imagery, & Wordplay

Welcome to the land of symbols, imagery, and wordplay. Before you travel any further, please know that there may be some thorny academic terminology ahead. Never fear, Shmoop is here. Check out our "How to Read a Poem" section for a glossary of terms.

Frà Pandolf's Painting of the Duchess

The most obvious symbol in "My Last Duchess" is the one that the Duke spends most of his time talking about – the portrait of the Duchess painted by Frà Pandolf on the wall of his private

gallery. Intriguingly, the Duke doesn't say much about the painting itself, except that it's lifelike and that it seems to capture the Duchess's emotional state. We don't get any sense of what pose the Duchess is in, what she's wearing, or what the color scheme or brushstrokes. What we do learn about the painting is that it's painted directly on the gallery wall, and so the Duke has to keep it covered by a curtain so that he can control who views it.

- Lines 1-2: The Duke points toward the portrait of the duchess using the language of this first sentence – "that" and "painted on the wall" start setting the scene for the reader.
- Lines 3-4: When the Duke describes the hard work that went into the painting of the Duchess, he uses a synecdoche, making Frà Pandolf's hands, not Frà Pandolf himself, the subject of the sentence. By reducing the painter to the part of his body that does the work, he dehumanizes Frà Pandolf, turning him into a tool instead of a person.
- Line 8: It's a tough call on this one, but you could think of the painting of the Duchess as personified. After all, paintings themselves are just paint on a surface, but this painting is looking at the viewer – it has an "earnest glance" – and it almost seems like it has feelings – "depth and passion." However, because the painting is an image of a person, you could also interpret the Duke's comments as being about the subject of the painting, instead of the painting itself – in which case this wouldn't be personification.
- Lines 17-19: Imagining the way the painter might have complimented the Duchess, the Duke uses elaborate imagery.

That Spot of Joy

When the Duchess is happy about something – and we really mean anything, her marriage, her dinner, the weather, anything at all – she smiles and blushes, and the Duke describes her blush s a "spot of joy" (21) that appears in her cheek. The spot of joy is an involuntary signal of the Duchess's pleasure, something that she can't control, that betrays her inner feelings to the world. The Duke thinks of it as a "spot" – a stain, a symbol of her tainted nature.

- Lines 13-15: The Duke uses a tongue-in-cheek understatement to emphasize how many things cause the "spot of joy" to appear in the Duchess's cheek.
- The phrase "spot of joy" itself is a startling juxtaposition of images that makes the reader think differently about the kind of blush that crosses the face of the Duchess. The fact that her blushing is referred to as a "spot" makes it sound blameworthy.
- Lines 21-22: In order to convey that he perceives the Duchess as flirtatious, the Duke comes up with a euphemism – "too soon made glad," which is a roundabout way of saying "easily pleased" – or maybe just "easy."
- Of course, that may not be an accurate characterization of the Duchess – but that's how the Duke perceives her. Since the Duchess isn't here to defend herself, all we have to go on is the Duke's claim.

Smiles

Along with blushes, the Duchess bestows pleased smiles on anyone and anything that brings a little bit of joy into her life. The Duke thinks of these smiles almost the way you might think of

collector's items – they're worth less (maybe even worthless) because she gives out so many of them. In fact, it seems like the Duke thinks that the Duchess should only smile for him. Taking pleasure in your life, let alone in its subtle details, just doesn't fit with his prestige-and-power philosophy.

- Lines 23-24: The Duke continues to use indirect language and figures of speech to imply that the Duchess is too flirtatious without saying so directly.
- In these lines, he uses innuendo together with metonymy – "her looks went everywhere" – to suggest that she herself "goes everywhere" too. (An *innuendo* is a seemingly innocent statement that implies something bawdy, sexy, or racy. Basically, anything you could follow with "nudge, nudge" or "that's what she said" counts as an innuendo.)
- Lines 31-34: The Duchess isn't the only one reduced to an intangible thing associated with her – the Duke describes his marriage to her using metonymy, calling it the "gift" of his "nine-hundred-years-old name."
- Lines 43-45: The Duke asks a rhetorical question, implying that the Duchess bestows the same smile on everyone around her.
- Line 46: The Duke uses synecdoche when he admits to his murder of the Duchess; instead of saying that he killed her, he mentions that all of her smiles have stopped.

Stooping

It's important to notice that when the Duke describes something that he thinks of as inappropriate or base for him to do, he does so by calling it "stooping." He considers himself to be on a high social pedestal, with his "nine-hundred-years-old name" and his wealth. He can't "lower" himself, even to tell someone that he's angry with them. Normal communication and behavior are out of the question for him, because they fall into the category of "stooping."

- Lines 34-35: The Duke uses a rhetorical question to force his listener to agree with him that it would be "stooping" to talk to the Duchess directly about her inappropriate behavior.
- Line 36: A paradox: the Duke claims that he doesn't have "skill in speech," even though he's speaking skillfully in order to say so!
- Lines 42-43: In these lines, as the Duke repeats his belief that communicating with the Duchess would be "stooping," Browning uses assonance, or the repetition of vowel sounds, to bring emphasis to the lines.

Neptune Taming a Seahorse

The final art object that the Duke points out to the Count's servant as they leave his gallery is a bronze statue of Neptune, the Roman god of the sea, taming a seahorse. The Duke emphasizes that this statue was cast for him specifically and names the sculptor, Claus of Innsbruck – which presumably means that this sculptor is well-known. As readers, we have to consider this statue as a foil to the only other art object that we see in the gallery – the portrait of the Duchess.

- Lines 54-56: Browning uses alliteration and consonance to unify and structure the lines

describing the statue of Neptune.

Form and Meter

Iambic Pentameter Couplets

Browning himself described this poem as a "dramatic lyric" – at least, *Dramatic Lyrics* was the title he gave to the book of poems in which "My Last Duchess" first appeared. The "dramatic" part of the poem is obvious: it has fictional characters who act out a scene.

The "lyric" part is less clear. "My Last Duchess" doesn't read like a typical lyric poem. Its rhymed iambic pentameter lines, like its dramatic setup, remind us of Shakespeare's plays and other Elizabethan drama. But it is about the inner thoughts of an individual speaker, instead of a dialogue between more than one person. That makes it more like the Romantic lyrics that came before it in the early part of the nineteenth century – stuff by Wordsworth, Coleridge, and Shelley that are all about the mind of the individual. So, really, Browning's title *Dramatic Lyrics* says it all. "My Last Duchess" is what would happen if Shakespeare's *Macbeth* married Wordsworth's "Tintern Abbey" and they had a baby. It's a hybrid of a play and a poem – a "dramatic lyric."

As for meter, "My Last Duchess" uses the rhythm called "iambic pentameter." *Iambic* means that the rhythm is based on two-syllable units in which the first syllable is . . . oh, drat, your eyes are glazing over. Stay with us here. Okay, an iamb goes "da DUM," like that. *Pentameter* means that there are five ("penta") of those in a line. Listen: "There's MY last DUCHess HANGing ON the WALL" – that's iambic pentameter. Okay, okay, you could argue that "on" shouldn't be stressed and so forth, but that's the basic idea.

Why does this matter? Well, for one thing, some people like to claim that iambic pentameter is the most "natural" rhythm for the English language to fall into, and that we often speak in iambic pentameter without noticing. Nobody's ever really been able to prove this, and probably nobody ever will, but it's a persistent "myth" about meter, so you should know it's out there. It also means that lines written in iambic pentameter feel conversational to us. If you listen to someone read "My Last Duchess" aloud (check out our "Links" section for some online audio recordings by contemporary poets and scholars), you might not even notice that it has a fancy meter, because it sounds more like normal speech than some other poetry does.

The other thing about iambic pentameter, like we said before, is that Shakespeare and other Elizabethan dramatists used it in their plays. Browning, a very highly educated writer, knew this, and his decision to use this meter in a poem that already feels sort of like a play is a direct allusion to the patterns of monologues (speeches made to others) and soliloquies (speeches made while alone) in drama. "My Last Duchess" is more of a monologue than a soliloquy, because there is a character listening to the Duke in the poem. He's *not* speaking his thoughts aloud to himself while he's alone, the way Hamlet does.

Of course, although the iambic rhythm makes us think of Elizabethan drama, the rhymed couplets (pairs of rhymed lines that occur together) of the poem keep tying the Duke's speech into tidy packages, even though his thoughts and sentences are untidy. Both Shakespeare and the great Romantic poet William Wordsworth used iambic pentameter without rhyme, a form called blank verse. But Browning introduces couplets into the mix. We think you can probably guess why it might be more appropriate for the control-freak Duke of Ferrara to speak in harsh, structured, rhymed lines than in unrhymed ones.

Speaker

The Duke of Ferrara

The speaker of "My Last Duchess" is, of course, the Duke of Ferrara. But it's important to think about him, not only as a character, but as a speaker. We need to consider his rhetoric, and syntax, and speech patterns. We know what kind of a man the Duke is, but what kind of an orator is he?

First of all, the Duke's speech is highly formalized, using strict rhyme and meter to organize itself into couplets (AABBCC etc.). He's a man who appreciates control, and he takes pains to control his own statements. But the syntax, or sentence structure, of the poem pulls against its rhyme scheme. The lines are paired in rhymed couplets, but these couplets are "open" – that is, the sentences don't finish at the same time the lines do. For example:

> *I repeat,*
> *The Count your master's known munificence*
> *Is ample warrant that no just pretense*
> *Of mine for dowry will be disallowed;*
> *Though his fair daughter's self, as I avowed*
> *At starting, is my object. (48-53)*

This statement is one sentence and contains two couplets, but the sense of the lines continually spills past the rhyming words. The Duke can shape his speech into couplets, but his thoughts strain against that structure and try to break it. There's a sense of struggle in his lines, as though he's just barely managing to rein things in and about to lose it at any moment. Given what happened to his "last Duchess," we're frightened of what will happen when he finally loses control.

Sound Check

"My Last Duchess" reminds us of an arrogant speech by a witty guy who knows he's witty. Because it's written in iambic pentameter, and because it has so many dramatic qualities, it reminds us of a Shakespeare play. We imagine the most pompous actor we've ever seen standing in the middle of a stage, planting his feet wide apart, and declaiming his lines with a lot of pretentious self-importance. There's no doubt that the Duke is self-important. After all, what

makes him angry about the last Duchess's behavior is that she thinks anyone could be important *as important* as he is. Toward the end of the poem, as the Duke walks his listener downstairs toward the rest of the party, he points out one last piece of art in his collection:

> *Notice Neptune, though,*
> *Taming a sea-horse, thought a rarity,*
> *Which Claus of Innsbruck cast in bronze for me! (54-56)*

We can just see the Duke pointing proudly at the statue, speaking each of his phrases with distinction, and crackling those hard consonants ("Which *C*laus of Innsbru*ck c*ast in bronze for me!") for all he's worth.

What's Up With the Title?

The title of "My Last Duchess," like the first few lines of the poem, gives us quite a bit of information about the dramatic scenario in the text. The word "My" clues us in to the fact that the poem is going to be in the first-person – so, before the poem even begins, we know from the title that we're going to be hearing the voice of a character, not just of a general poetic speaker. The title "Duchess" makes it clear that we're dealing with European nobility, probably in a bygone age. And then there's that adjective "last."

We'll go ahead and ask the obvious question for you: why is she the Duke's last Duchess? Well, that implies that there will be another Duchess in the future – and that there might have been several Duchesses before her. But wait a minute, isn't marriage forever? Not for this Duke, who seems to dispose of Duchesses pretty quickly. So the designation "last" implies that this Duchess is only one of a sequence, preparing us for the fact that the poem might consider some of the other women who end up in that sequence.

After all, when you start describing something as your "last" one, you're usually about to start explaining what's going to be different about your "next" one, as in "My last car always hydroplaned, but I'm going to make sure my next one has good traction." The Duke's last Duchess smiled and showed favors to everyone, and the Duke is going to make sure that his next wife, the daughter of the Count, doesn't behave in the same way. How is he going to do that? Well, telling this story to her father's servant, and thereby warning everyone in the Count's household that he murders wives who are nice to their servants and male friends, is probably a pretty good start.

Calling Card

A Psychopath Pouring Out His Heart

If you enjoyed the chance to get inside the head of a jealous madman in "My Last Duchess," you're in luck: Browning several different poems, many of them dramatic monologues, in which he assumes the voice of a psychopathic speaker. As in "My Last Duchess," Browning tends to balance his complete immersion in the voice and mind of the madman with his own subtle moral

perspective on the poem. If you want to hear the voice of a man who strangles his lover with her own hair, or a masochistic self-proclaimed saint, or a monk who plots the demise of one of his fellow brothers, Browning is the author for you. We recommend you read "Porphyria's Lover," "St. Simeon Stylites," and "Soliloquy of the Spanish Cloister" next. Oh, and don't plan to read any of them over a meal, either. Unless you want to get sick.

Tough-O-Meter

(3) Base Camp

As nineteenth-century poems go, this certainly isn't the toughest thing you're going to encounter. It's pretty conversational – in fact, it's half of a conversation. You can easily imagine that you're the servant sitting in the Duke's private gallery, listening to him talk about when and how the portrait was painted and what makes him such a jealous psychopath. The most difficult thing about the poem is the syntax, the order of words and phrases that the Duke uses. For example:

> *I said*
> *"Frà Pandolf" by design, for never read*
> *Strangers like you that pictured countenance,*
> *The depth and passion of its earnest glance,*
> *But to myself they turned (since none puts by*
> *The curtain I have drawn for you, but I)*
> *And seemed as they would ask me, if they durst,*
> *How such a glance came there; so, not the first*
> *Are you to turn and ask thus. (5-13)*

We count nine different phrases and clauses in that nine-line sentence, including the parenthetical aside, just so the Duke can say, "I brought up that guy Pandolf on purpose, because people always want to ask me who painted the picture." Passages like this are especially strange because the Duke can be concise and to the point when he wants to be: "This grew; I gave commands; / Then all smiles stopped together" (45-46). That's the shortest way of saying "So, her behavior became even more extreme, and I decided that I would have her murdered" that we've ever heard.

Why so much variation in the length and complexity of the sentences? Well, for one thing, it makes the poem more interesting than if every sentence was exactly one or two lines long. But it also lets us gauge the Duke's mood and mania. In the shorter sentences where the Duke is to the point, we can imagine him being steely and strong: "I gave commands." No compromises there. But in the longer, more tortured sentences with wacky syntax, we might wonder exactly why it's so hard for him to say these particular things in a straightforward way, and what other details are creeping into the sentence that don't need to be there.

In the long passage we quoted above, what the Duke is trying to say is just "People always ask me who painted the picture and how they made it so lifelike," but he ends up also mentioning

that he insists on having total control over the painting. Our point is that, when this poem gets difficult to understand, that's when you should start looking for several levels of information coming from the Duke – the things he's trying to say, the things he lets slip on purpose, and the things he lets slip by accident.

Setting

A Private Art Gallery in the Palace of the Duke of Ferrara

Unlike some lyric poetry, and very much like a play, "My Last Duchess" has a very definite physical and geographical setting: a private art gallery in the palace of the Duke of Ferrara in mid-sixteenth-century Renaissance Italy. The modern day country of Italy didn't exist during the Renaissance – the many city-states in the region weren't unified until the late nineteenth century. But Ferrara was a city-state in what is today northern Italy, sort of near Bologna. Browning even tells us this setting in the epigraph, as though he were listing the location of the scene in a play. What's interesting is that the real historical details of life in sixteenth-century Ferrara are much less important to the poem than the connotations and stereotypes of an Italian Renaissance palace.

Browning was writing for a nineteenth-century audience (even if that audience didn't always "get" his poetry), and that nineteenth-century audience would have immediately made certain assumptions about a place like Ferrara. You know how, if we say "Transylvania," you immediately think of Dracula, werewolves, and creepy moonlit castles? Well, for nineteenth-century British readers, saying "Renaissance Italy" would have made them think of fantastic art objects, extravagant living, lavish palaces, and sinister political ideas of the Machiavelli sort. In this way, that simple epigraph "Ferrara" suggests a whole cluster of themes – even if some of those themes might be inaccurate stereotypes.

Themes

Theme of Power

"My Last Duchess" is all about power: the political and social power wielded by the speaker (the Duke) and his attempt to control the domestic sphere (his marriage) in the same way that he rules his lands. He rules with an iron fist. The Duke views everything that he possesses and everyone with whom he interacts as an opportunity to expand his power base. Wives need to be dominated; servants need to understand his authority; and fancy objects in his art gallery display his influence to the world – if he decides to show them. Kindness, joy, and emotion are all threats to his tyrannical power.

Questions About Power

1. How does the Duke want the people around him, such as his "last Duchess" and the

servant of the Count who listens to her story, to respond to his power? How does he attempt to shape their reactions?

2. What do the Duke's brief asides to his listener show us about the way he manages his power? (Think especially of lines 5, 47-48, and 53-54.)

3. Why does the Duke think that it would be "stooping" to explain to the Duchess why he dislikes her smiling and blushing? In his mind, how would talking to her about these issues compromise his position of power?

4. What powers does the Duchess have? What aspects of her life – including her husband's behavior and her own – is she unable to control?

Chew on this: Power

The Duke of Ferrara sets himself up to have his power threatened, because he never communicates directly with people about his expectations for their behavior.

Theme of Language and Communication

In "My Last Duchess," choices about what to communicate and what to withhold are the means by which power is wielded. The Duke sees communicating openly and honestly with someone about the problems you have with their behavior as impossible because it would compromise his authority. It's also possible to hint at his power by intentionally letting stories of the past exploits slip to a new listener. However, because language is full of subtlety, the Duke might accidentally communicate more than he meant to about his own psychosis.

Questions About Language and Communication

1. The Duke claims that he doesn't have "skill in speech" to make his "will clear" to the Duchess. Is he right? Does he display any evidence of rhetorical skill in the poem itself? If so, then why couldn't he communicate with the Duchess?

2. Why does the Duke think that it would be "stooping" to communicate his thoughts and feelings to the Duchess? Why doesn't telling the story to his listener count as "stooping," too? What makes retelling the story to a third party different?

3. What is the Duke really hoping to communicate by telling the story of his "last Duchess" to the Count's servant? Who is meant to receive the message?

4. What does the Duke communicate about himself unintentionally by retelling the story of his murder of the Duchess? How do these unintended meanings slip through the language of the poem?

Chew on this: Language and Communication

The Duke is only able to describe his maniacal feelings to someone who is not the object of those feelings.

Theme of Art and Culture

"My Last Duchess" is a piece of art about a piece of (fictional) art – a poem about a pretend painting. The speaker of the poem, the Duke of Ferrara, is a connoisseur and collector of *objets d'art* , or art objects, which he displays privately in order to impress people. In this poem, art and culture become tools for demonstrating social status – and ways to reduce unstable elements, like the Duchess herself, to things that can be physically controlled.

Questions About Art and Culture

1. Why does the Duke have a private art gallery? To whom do you think he usually shows the objects in his collection?
2. Why is there a curtain over the portrait of the "last Duchess"? (Hint: can the portrait be moved?)
3. Why is it so important that the portrait of the Duchess is full-length and extremely lifelike? How does the replacement of the real Duchess with her portrait work? What does the Duke gain by this replacement? What does he lose?
4. How does the bronze statue of Neptune taming a seahorse relate to the portrait of the Duchess? Why does the Duke make a point of showing this second object to the Count's servant?

Chew on this: Art and Culture

Even though the Duke is a collector of art objects, he doesn't really appreciate them; he only cares about the way they increase his status and demonstrate his power.

Theme of Madness

In "My Last Duchess," a husband murders his wife because she blushes and smiles at other people – even though theses blushes are out of her control and probably entirely innocent. This is pretty much the textbook definition of an abusive, controlling husband. The Duke doesn't even want his wife to thank people for gifts, because it makes him jealous. But we think this goes beyond abuse into the realm of madness: after all, trying to control someone is abuse; thinking that because someone blushes she must be having an affair, and that the only remedy is murder is just insane.

Questions About Madness

1. Is the Duke actually crazy? Which aspects of his speech and behavior suggest that he's a psychopath? Which suggest that he's sane but cruel?
2. Does the Duke seem capable of analyzing his own behavior? That is, does he hint that he

knows how extreme his actions are?

3. What does the Duke disclose to his listener without intending to do so? How do these disclosures change our opinion of his sanity or insanity?

Chew on this: Madness

The Duke's obsession with totalitarian power, and his tendency to punish innocent or nearly innocent behavior with the most extreme penalties, make it clear that he's a psychopath.

Theme of Jealousy

The Duke in "My Last Duchess" is pretty much the green-eyed monster incarnate. He's almost an allegorical figure for jealousy. He's jealous of the attention his wife shows to other people – even if all she does is thank them for bringing her some cherries. He's jealous of every smile and every blush that she bestows, intentionally or unintentionally, on someone else. He's so jealous that he can't even bring himself to talk to her about her behavior – murder is the only solution he can come up with. His jealousy isn't just about romantic attention; it's about any kind of attention.

Questions About Jealousy

1. What evidence can you find in the poem to suggest that the Duke suspects the Duchess of having, or at least seeming to have, a lover? Is there any evidence that she's actually having an affair? Does that matter to the Duke?
2. Why is the Duke jealous of the smiles and thanks that the Duchess shows to other people? Does he actually value her smiles and thanks? Does he want her to give all her admiration to him, or to stifle her admiring behavior entirely?
3. When the Duke imagines different ways of telling the Duchess about his jealousy, he comes up with "here you miss, / Or there exceed the mark" (38-39). What is "the mark"? How does the Duke use "the mark" to judge the Duchess's behavior? Is the mark at all related to the "spot of joy" (21)?

Chew on this: Jealousy

The Duke is jealous of the way the Duchess treats other people, not because he loves her and wants all her love for himself, but because he wants her to acknowledge his power over her.

Quotes

Power Quotes

(since none puts by
The curtain I have drawn for you, but I) (9-10)

Thought: The Duke's first allusion to the great power he wields comes in a parenthetical aside, in which he lets slip, intentionally or unintentionally, that he alone controls access to his late wife's portrait. Even her image is under his jealous guard. The words "control freak" come to mind.

She thanked men, – good! but thanked
Somehow – I know not how – as if she ranked
My gift of a nine-hundred-years-old name
With anybody's gift. (31-34)

Thought: The Duke's emphasis on his family history and prestige – his "nine-hundred-years-old name" – is underscored by his choice of the word "ranked" to describe the way people should react to gifts. When was the last time you came up with a hierarchy of your birthday presents?

– E'en then would be some stooping; and I choose
Never to stoop. (42-43)

Thought: Maintaining his own stiff-upper-lip dignity is more important to the Duke than dropping the Duchess a few hints that, if she doesn't start being a bit less happy-go-lucky, he's going to have her killed. "Stooping" would be a more serious threat to his power than her flirtatious nature.

This grew; I gave commands;
Then all smiles stopped together. (45-46)

Thought: Not only does the Duke have the power to order someone killed, he doesn't do his dirty work himself. He only has to give "commands" – he can just pick up the red phone and things get done. This emphasizes how far up the social ladder he is – but it also suggests that he's dependent on underlings. We're not sure the snobby Duke has it in him to kill somebody with his own two hands.

Nay, we'll go
Together down, sir. (53-54)

Thought: The Duke is obsessed with power in every relationship – not only in a major relationship like his marriage, but also in the minor relationship between him and his listener, the servant of the Count. When the servant tries to get away from him after hearing the story of the Duchess, the Duke insists that they head back to the party together. Not only does this show how the Duke can control every little move the servant makes, it prevents the servant from telling the Count what he's heard privately – which might make the Count back out on the marriage between his daughter and the Duke.

Language and Communication Quotes

never read
Strangers like you that pictured countenance,
The depth and passion of its earnest glance,
But to myself they turned . . .
And seemed as they would ask me, if they durst,
How such a glance came there (6-9, 11-12)

Thought: There are several different kinds of communication happening here. The Duke is telling the servant a story about the portrait of the Duchess. But he's also picking up on the nonverbal cues that tell him what question the servant wants to ask. (Although he may be projecting that desire onto the servant; we can't be sure, because we don't get any information in the poem about how the servant is actually reacting.) The Duke also inadvertently implies that he's used to people being afraid of him – they want to ask about the portrait, but they don't dare.

all and each
Would draw from her alike the approving speech,
Or blush, at least. (29-31)

Thought: The Duke's big problem with the Duchess is that the way she communicates with people isn't nuanced enough. She gives the same friendly, flirty reaction to everyone and everything.

Even had you skill
In speech – (which I have not) – to make your will
Quite clear to such an one (35-37)

Thought: The Duke claims that he can't talk to the Duchess about her behavior because he's not a good enough speaker to really make his feelings clear to her. But we can tell this is just an excuse, because the language he uses to describe the situation to the Count's servant is quite skillful.

This grew; I gave commands;
Then all smiles stopped together. (45-46)

Thought: Although the Duke doesn't want to communicate with the Duchess directly about her indiscriminate kindness, he sets up an alternate, indirect line of communication in order to bring about her murder. This other path of communication depends on an underling who will hear and carry out the Duke's orders. The implied murder of the Duchess turns the Duke's commands into performative language.

Art and Culture Quotes

I call
That piece a wonder, now: Frà Pandolf's hands
Worked busily a day, and there she stands. (2-4)

Thought: Notice that the first comment the Duke makes about his late wife's portrait is that it is successful as a piece of art – it's realistic, lifelike, and shows the painter's skill. This artistic quality is far more important to him than any sentimental value. (We're not sure the Duke has sentiment anyway.)

that pictured countenance,
The depth and passion of its earnest glance (7-8)

Thought: The portrait of the Duchess seems to have captured her spirit. The Duke doesn't describe the portrait in terms of its artistic school, colors, shapes, or brushstrokes – he describes its emotional quality.

"Paint
Must never hope to reproduce the faint
Half-flush that dies along her throat:" (17-19)

Thought: The Duke imagines the painter, Frà Pandolf, complimenting the Duchess by telling her that no artistic medium could actually reproduce the complex flushes and tints of her skin. In the Duke's opinion, there is no greater compliment than the suggestion that a human being could be superior to an art object.

Too easily impressed: she liked whate'er
She looked on, and her looks went everywhere. (23-24)

Thought: The Duke's assessment of the Duchess is that she likes everything in the same way indiscriminately. As a connoisseur and collector, he values the ability to make fine distinctions between the quality of different objects or acts. The Duchess's general appreciation of everything – and everyone – in the same way frustrates him to no end. It's important to notice

that part of his objection to her behavior is that she isn't critical or analytic about things the way he is.

There she stands
As if alive. (46-47)

Thought: This is a simple but deceptive statement, which emphasizes several things including: the lifelike quality of the painting, the fact that the Duchess is no longer alive, and the idea that Frà Pandolf's painting might replace the real-life Duchess for the Duke.

Notice Neptune, though,
Taming a sea-horse, thought a rarity,
Which Claus of Innsbruck cast in bronze for me! (54-56)

Thought: At the end of the poem, the Duke concludes his monologue by pointing out one more art object in his gallery – a statue of Neptune, the god of the sea, taming a seahorse. It's important to him to emphasize the name of the artist and that the piece was commissioned especially for him. (Notice his use of the exclamation point, a rare occurrence in the poem.)We suspect it might also be important to him that the subject of the piece is taming – he seems to enjoy domesticating and dominating other people.

Madness Quotes
THAT'S my last Duchess painted on the wall,
Looking as if she were alive. (1-2)

Thought: The Duke knows the difference between the living Duchess and her painting – but he doesn't *see* it as much of a difference. It's startling that he brings up the unusual circumstances of his previous wife's death at the beginning of this conversation with a servant of the family he wants to marry into next. He's a little bit obsessive to say the least.

as if she ranked
My gift of a nine-hundred-years-old name
With anybody's gift. Who'd stoop to blame
This sort of trifling? (32-35)

Thought: The Duke can't believe that anyone would fail to understand that the most important thing in the universe is having an old family name. Again, this isn't exactly insanity, but it is an extremely narrow-minded attitude toward values.

"Just this
Or that in you disgusts me; here you miss,
Or there exceed the mark" (37-39)

Thought: OK, at this point, we're really starting to wonder about the Duke's sanity. "Disgust" is a bizarrely strong and inappropriate word to use to describe your reaction to someone smiling when they ride their white mule. If the Duke is this inappropriate with his word choice, we have to wonder about the other ways in which he is inappropriate.

This grew; I gave commands;
Then all smiles stopped together. There she stands
As if alive. Will't please you rise? We'll meet
The company below, then. (45-48)

Thought: This is the point where we become pretty sure that the Duke is a little unhinged. Admitting that you had your wife murdered is one thing – politely asking your guest to walk downstairs in the very next sentence is psychotic.

Jealousy Quotes

Sir, 'twas not
Her husband's presence only, called that spot
Of joy into the Duchess' cheek (13-15)

Thought: The Duke is offended that the Duchess would take pleasure in anything other than him. Notice that the way she shows her pleasure is involuntary, (i.e., a blush counts as showing pleasure), but the Duke describes it as though it were a stain or taint, a "*spot* of joy."

perhaps
Frà Pandolf chanced to say, "Her mantle laps
Over my lady's wrist too much," or "Paint
Must never hope to reproduce the faint
Half-flush that dies along her throat" (15-19)

Thought: The Duke's jealous fantasies are very elaborate – he's imagined in detail the kind of compliments that the painter might have paid to the Duchess, and the coy way that she might have responded. It's important to remember that, as far as we know, this could all be in his head. There's no evidence in the poem that the painter said these things or that the Duchess blushed in response.

such stuff
Was courtesy, she thought, and cause enough
For calling up that spot of joy. (19-21)

Thought: The Duke seems to believe that the Duchess *chooses* to blush or react to compliments and gifts. He describes her as "calling up" her blushes, instead of experiencing them as an involuntary reaction. As readers, we know that she probably isn't blushing intentionally, and the Duke's jealousy is illogical.

She had
A heart – how shall I say? – too soon made glad.
Too easily impressed: she liked whate'er
She looked on, and her looks went everywhere. (21-24)

Thought: When was the last time you heard someone complain because their spouse found joy and pleasure in too many things? "Man, I can't stand my wife, she's happy all the time," you might imagine the Duke saying. The Duke fantasizes that this pleasure in the world implies that his wife is promiscuous – a stretch, to say the least.

Oh sir, she smiled, no doubt,
Whene'er I passed her; but who passed without
Much the same smile? (43-5)

Thought: The Duke thinks of kindness as less valuable if it isn't selective. As he portrays her, the Duchess is a kind and attentive wife to him, but that means less, in his mind, because she's kind and attentive to everyone. He wants her to save all her affection for him alone – classic controlling abusive husband stuff.

Study Questions

1. Would you be willing to marry the Duke of Ferrara?
2. What else do you think the Duke might have in his gallery, besides the portrait of the Duchess and the bronze statue of Neptune taming a seahorse?
3. Is it significant that the portrait of the Duchess is painted on the wall, instead of on a canvas? Why might a painter work directly on the surface of the wall, instead of on a surface that could be moved?
4. Why doesn't the Duke tell the Duchess directly that her behavior annoys him? What exactly does the Duchess do that drives him so wild?
5. Why does the Duke tell this story about his "last Duchess" to the servant of the man whose daughter he hopes to marry next?
6. Why are the only two named people in the poem, Frà Pandolf and Claus of Innsbruck, painters?

Did You Know?

Trivia

- During his marriage, Robert Browning often took a back seat to his much more famous wife, Elizabeth Barrett Browning, whose verse novels *Aurora Leigh* and *Sonnets from the Portuguese* catapulted her to fame. Some Victorian readers even referred to Robert as "Mrs. Browning's husband." (Source)
- "My Last Duchess" is often compared to another of Robert Browning's poems, "Porphyria's Lover," another dramatic monologue in which a psychopathic speaker explains what drove him to murder his significant other. (Source)
- In 1889, Robert Browning was recorded reciting his poem "How They Brought the Good News from Ghent to Aix" – and forgetting some of the words. This recording is one of the first audio recordings of any human voice. (Source)
- Robert Browning is the author of one of the most famous English-language versions of the story of the Pied Piper of Hamelin. (Source)

Steaminess Rating

PG

Nobody has sex in "My Last Duchess." Instead we get to watch the Duke of Ferrara writhing as he talks about his paranoid suspicion that his wife is having an affair. Even something as harmless as a blush or a "spot of joy" in her cheek makes him gnash his teeth. His murderous jealousy seems creepily sexual when we remember that he's telling the story as part of the wooing process for his next wife.

Allusions and Cultural References

Mythological References

- Neptune (54)

Historical References

- Ferrara (epigraph)

Best of the Web

Videos
"My Last Duchess" Amateur Video
http://www.youtube.com/watch?v=5wON8-glDb0
In this amateur video, two men enact the dramatic relationship between the Duke of Ferrara and the servant who listens to his monologue. "My Last Duchess" is an especially good poem to see acted out, because as a dramatic monologue it's much like a short excerpt from a play.

"My Last Duchess" Reading
http://www.youtube.com/watch?v=3Irb-P1nDAE&feature=related
A solid reading of the poem complements a portrait reminiscent of Browning's Duchess.

Audio
Richard Howard's Reading of "My Last Duchess"
http://poets.org/viewmedia.php/prmMID/15701
An audio reading of Browning's poem by contemporary poet Richard Howard.

Images
Robert Browning
http://dept.kent.edu/IBEWebsite/images/brown.jpg
Image of the young Robert Browning.

Websites
"My Last Duchess" at Representative Poetry Online
http://rpo.library.utoronto.ca/poem/288.html
This site, run by the University of Toronto Library, includes full text of the poem, footnotes, and commentary by Ian Lancashire. A great place to begin your research.

Robert Browning on The Victorian Web
http://www.victorianweb.org/authors/rb/rbov.html
Articles, background, and analysis on Browning from a variety of eminent scholars.

Biography of Robert Browning
http://www.poets.org/poet.php/prmPID/182
A short, scholarly, citable description of Browning's background, marriage, and career.

Historical Documents

Robert Browning's Obituary
http://query.nytimes.com/gst/abstract.html?res=9E01E0DF1E30E633A25750C1A9649D94689F
D7CF
This obituary notice from the *New York Times* appeared on December 13, 1889.

Books

The Poetic and Dramatic Works of Robert Browning
http://books.google.com/books?id=et0gAAAAMAAJ&printsec=frontcover&dq=inauthor:%22Rob
ert+Browning%22#PPP1,M1
This edition is a free e-book available on Google Books. Note: this is not a complete edition of
all Browning's poetry – there's way more out there!

Selected Poems of Robert Browning
http://www.amazon.com/Selected-Penguin-Classics-Robert-Browning/dp/0140437266
This Penguin edition of Browning's poetry includes all the most important poems and has good,
authoritative footnotes – but only a small sample is available in the free online preview.

Robert Browning's Poetry
http://www.amazon.com/Robert-Brownings-Poetry-Critical-Editions/dp/0393926001/ref=sr_1_1?
ie=UTF8&s=books&qid=1222311316&sr=8-1
This Norton Critical edition of Browning's poetry also includes several interesting critical
essays. No online preview available.

Movies & TV

The Barretts of Wimpole Street
http://www.imdb.com/title/tt0024865/
This Oscar-nominated classic film from 1934 dramatizes the real-life love story of Elizabeth
Barrett and Robert Browning.

Shmoop's Poetry Primer

How to Read Poem

There's really only one reason that poetry has gotten a reputation for being so darned
"difficult": it demands your full attention and won't settle for less. Unlike a novel, where you can
drift in and out and still follow the plot, poems are generally shorter and more intense, with less
of a conventional story to follow. If you don't make room for the *experience*, you probably
won't have one.

But the rewards can be high. To make an analogy with rock and roll, it's the difference between
a two and a half minute pop song with a hook that you get sick of after the third listen, and a
slow-building tour de force that sounds fresh and different every time you hear it. Once you've
gotten a taste of the really rich stuff, you just want to listen to it over and over again and figure

out: how'd they do that?

Aside from its demands on your attention, there's nothing too tricky about reading a poem. Like anything, it's a matter of practice. But in case you haven't read much (or any) poetry before, we've put together a short list of tips that will make it a whole lot more enjoyable.

- **Follow Your Ears.** It's okay to ask, "What does it mean?" when reading a poem. But it's even better to ask, "How does it sound?" If all else fails, treat it like a song. Even if you can't understand a single thing about a poem's "subject" or "theme," you can always say something – anything – about the sound of the words. Does the poem move fast or slow? Does it sound awkward in sections or does it have an even flow? Do certain words stick out more than others? Trust your inner ear: if the poem sounds strange, it doesn't mean you're reading it wrong. In fact, you probably just discovered one of the poem's secret tricks! If you get stuck at any point, just look for Shmoop's "Sound Check" section. We'll help you listen!

- **Read It Aloud.** OK, we're not saying you have to shout it from the rooftops. If you're embarrassed and want to lock yourself in the attic and read the poem in the faintest whisper possible, go ahead. Do whatever it takes, because reading even part of poem aloud can totally change your perspective on how it works.

- **Become an Archaeologist.** When you've drunk in the poem enough times, experiencing the sound and images found there, it is sometimes fun to switch gears and to become an archaeologist (you know -- someone who digs up the past and uncovers layers of history). Treat the poem like a room you have just entered. Perhaps it's a strange room that you've never seen before, filled with objects or people that you don't really recognize. Maybe you feel a bit like Alice in Wonderland. Assume your role as an archaeologist and take some measurements. What's the weather like? Are there people there? What kind of objects do you find? Are there more verbs than adjectives? Do you detect a rhythm? Can you hear music? Is there furniture? Are there portraits of past poets on the walls? Are there traces of other poems or historical references to be found? Check out Shmoop's "Setting," "Symbols, Imagery, Wordplay," and "Speaker" sections to help you get started.

- **Don't Skim.** Unlike the newspaper or a textbook, the point of poetry isn't to cram information into your brain. We can't repeat it enough: poetry is an experience. If you don't have the patience to get through a long poem, no worries, just start with a really short poem. Understanding poetry is like getting a suntan: you have to let it sink in. When you glance at Shmoop's "Detailed Summary," you'll see just how loaded each line of poetry can be.

- **Memorize!** "Memorize" is such a scary word, isn't it? It reminds us of multiplication tables. Maybe we should have said: "Tuck the poem into your snuggly memory-space." Or maybe not. At any rate, don't tax yourself: if you memorize one or two lines of a poem, or even just a single cool-sounding phrase, it will start to work on you in ways you didn't know possible. You'll be walking through the mall one day, and all of a sudden, you'll shout, "I get it!" Just not too loud, or you'll get mall security on your case.

- **Be Patient.** You can't really understand a poem that you've only read once. You just can't. So if you don't get it, set the poem aside and come back to it later. And by "later" we mean days, months, or even years. Don't rush it. It's a much bigger accomplishment to actually *enjoy* a poem than it is to be able to explain every line of it. Treat the first reading as an investment – your effort might not pay off until well into the future, but when it

does, it will totally be worth it. Trust us.

- **Read in Crazy Places.** Just like music, the experience of poetry changes depending on your mood and the environment. Read in as many different places as possible: at the beach, on a mountain, in the subway. Sometimes all it takes is a change of scenery for a poem to really come alive.

- **Think Like a Poet.** Here's a fun exercise. Go through the poem one line at a time, covering up the next line with your hand so you can't see it. Put yourself in the poet's shoes: If I had to write a line to come after this line, what would I put? If you start to think like this, you'll be able to appreciate all the different choices that go into making a poem. It can also be pretty humbling – at least we think so. Shmoop's "Calling Card" section will help you become acquainted with a poet's particular, unique style. Soon, you'll be able to decipher a T.S. Elliot poem from a Wallace Stevens poem, sight unseen. Everyone will be so jealous.

- **"Look Who's Talking."** Ask the most basic questions possible of the poem. Two of the most important are: "Who's talking?" and "Who are they talking to?" If it's a Shakespeare sonnet, don't just assume that the speaker is Shakespeare. The speaker of every poem is kind of fictional creation, and so is the audience. Ask yourself: what would it be like to meet this person? What would they look like? What's their "deal," anyway? Shmoop will help you get to know a poem's speaker through the "Speaker" section found in each study guide.

- And, most importantly, **Never Be Intimidated.** Regardless of what your experience with poetry in the classroom has been, no poet wants to make his or her audience feel stupid. It's just not good business, if you know what we mean. Sure, there might be tricky parts, but it's not like you're trying to unlock the secrets of the universe. Heck, if you want to ignore the "meaning" entirely, then go ahead. Why not? If you're still feeling a little timid, let Shmoop's "Why Should I Care" section help you realize just how much you have to bring to the poetry table.

Poetry is about freedom and exposing yourself to new things. In fact, if you find yourself stuck in a poem, just remember that the poet, 9 times out of 10, was a bit of a rebel and was trying to make his friends look at life in a completely different way. Find your inner rebel too. There isn't a single poem out there that's "too difficult" to try out – right now, today. So hop to it. As you'll discover here at Shmoop, there's plenty to choose from.

Sources:

http://allpoetry.com/column/2339540
http://academic.reed.edu/writing/paper_help/figurative_language.html
http://web.uvic.ca/wguide/Pages/LiteraryTermsTOC.html#RhetLang
http://www.tnellen.com/cybereng/lit_terms/allegory.html

What is Poetry?

What is poetry? At the most basic level, poetry is an *experience* produced by two elements of language: "sense" and "sound." The "sense" of a word is its meaning. The word "cat" refers to a small, furry animal with whiskers, a long tail, and, if you're unlucky, a knack for scratching up all your new furniture. We can all agree that's what "cat" means. But "cat" also has a particular sound when you say it, and this sound is different from similar words for "cat" in other languages.

Most of the things that you hear, say, or read in your daily life (including the words you are reading right now) put more emphasis on meaning than on sound. Not so with poetry. Have you ever repeated a word so many times that it started to sound strange and foreign? No? Try saying that word "cat" twenty times in a row. "Cat, cat, cat, cat, cat, cat . . ." Kind of weird, right? Well, guess what: you just made poetry out of a single word – that is, you turned the word into an experience that is as much about sound as it is about sense. Congratulations, poet!

Or let's imagine that you type the words "blue" and "ocean" on a page all by their lonesome selves. These two little words are quite ordinary and pop up in conversations all the time. However, when we see them isolated, all alone on a page, they might just take on a whole new meaning. Maybe "blue ocean" looks like a little strand of islands in a big sea of white space, and maybe we start to think about just how big the ocean is. Or you could reverse the order and type the words as "ocean blue," which would bring up a slightly different set of connotations, such as everyone's favorite grade-school rhyme: "In 1492 Columbus sailed the ocean blue."

Poetry is also visual, and so it's a good idea to pay attention to how the words are assembled on the page. Our imaginations are often stirred by a poem's visual presentation. Just like a person, poems can send all kinds of signals with their physical appearance. Some are like a slick businessman in a suit or a woman in an evening gown. Their lines are all regularized and divided neatly into even stanzas. Others are like a person at a rock concert who is dressed in tattered jeans, a ragged t-shirt, and a Mohawk, and who has tattoos and piercings all over their body! And some poems, well, some poems look like a <u>baked potato that exploded in your microwave</u>. It's always a good idea to ask yourself how the appearance of words on the page interacts with the meaning of those words. If the poem is about war, maybe it looks like a battle is going on, and the words are fighting for space. If the poem is about love, maybe the lines are spaced to appear as though they are dancing with one another. Often the appearance and meaning will be in total contrast, which is just as interesting.

OK, that's a very broad idea of what poetry is. Let's narrow it down a bit. When most people talk about poetry, they are talking about a particular kind of literature that is broken up into lines, or *verses*. In fact, for most of history, works divided into verse were considered more "literary" than works in prose. Even those long stories called "epics," like Homer's *The Odyssey* and Virgil's *Aeneid*, are actually poems.

Now, you're thinking: "Wait a minute, I thought verses belong to songs and music." Exactly. The very first poets – from Biblical times and even before – set their poems to music, and it's still acceptable to refer to a poem as a "song." For example, the most famous work by the

American poet Walt Whitman is titled, "Song of Myself." Because of their shared emphasis on sound, poetry and music have always been like blood brothers.

The last thing to say about poetry is that it doesn't like to be pinned down. That's why there's no single definition that fits all of the things that we would call "poems." Just when you think you have poetry cornered, and you're ready to define it as literature broken into lines, it breaks free and shouts, "Aha! You forgot about the *prose poem*, which doesn't have any verses!" Drats! Fortunately, we get the last laugh, because we can enjoy and recognize poems even without a perfect definition of what poetry is.

Sources:

http://allpoetry.com/column/2339540
http://academic.reed.edu/writing/paper_help/figurative_language.html
http://web.uvic.ca/wguide/Pages/LiteraryTermsTOC.html#RhetLang
http://www.tnellen.com/cybereng/lit_terms/allegory.html

Poetry Glossary

Allegory: An allegory is a kind of extended metaphor (a metaphor that weaves throughout the poem) in which objects, persons, and actions stand for another meaning.

Alliteration: Alliteration happens when words that begin with the same sound are placed close to one another. For example, "the **s**illy **s**nake **s**ilently **s**linked by" is a form of alliteration. Try saying that ten times fast.

Allusion: An allusion happens when a speaker or character makes a brief and casual reference to a famous historical or literary figure or event.

Anaphora: Anaphora involves the repetition of the same word or group of words at the beginning of successive clauses or sections. Think of an annoying kid on a road trip: "Are we there yet? / Are we going to stop soon? / Are we having lunch soon?". Not a poem we'd like to read in its entirety, but the repetition of the word "are" is anaphora.

Anthologize: To put in a poetry anthology, usually for teaching purposes, so that students have a broad selection of works to choose from. Usually, the word will come up in a context like this: "That's one of her most famous poems. I've seen it anthologized a lot." An anthology is a book that has samples of the work of a lot of different writers. It's like a plate of appetizers so you can try out a bunch of stuff. You can also find anthologies for different periods, like Romantic, Modern, and Postmodern. The Norton, Columbia, and Best American anthologies are three of the most famous.

Apostrophe: Apostrophe is when an idea, person, object, or absent being is addressed as if it

or they were present, alive, and kicking. John Donne uses apostrophe when he writes this: "Death be not proud, though some have called thee / Mighty and dreadful."

Avant Garde: You'll hear this word used to describe some of the craziest, most far-out, experimental poets. It was originally a French expression that refers to the soldiers who go explore a territory before the main army comes in. Avant garde artists are often people who break through boundaries and do what's never been done before. Then again, sometimes there's a good reason why something has been done before…

Ballad: A ballad is a song: think boy bands and chest-thumping emotion. But in poetry, a ballad is ancient form of storytelling. In the (very) old days, common people didn't get their stories from books – they were sung as musical poems. Because they are meant to convey information, ballads usually have a simple rhythm and a consistent rhyme scheme. They often tell the story of everyday heroes, and some poets, like Bob Dylan, continue to set them to music.

Blank Verse: Thanks to Shakespeare and others, blank verse is one of the most common forms of English poetry. It's verse that has no rhyme scheme but has a regular meter. Usually this meter is iambic pentameter (check out our definition below). Why is blank verse so common in English? Well, a lot of people think we speak in it in our everyday conversations. Kind of like we just did: "a LOT of PEO-ple THINK we SPEAK in IT." That could be a blank verse line.

Cadence: Cadence refers to the rhythmic or musical elements of a poem. You can think of it as the thing that makes poetry sound like poetry. Whereas "meter" refers to the regular elements of rhythm – the beats or accents – "cadence" refers to the momentary variations in rhythm, like when a line speeds up or slows down. Poets often repeat or contrast certain cadences to create a more interesting sound than normal prose.

Caesura: A fancy word for a pause that occurs in the middle of a line of verse. Use this if want to sound smart, but we think "pause" is just fine. You can create pauses in a lot of ways, but the most obvious is to use punctuation like a period, comma, or semicolon. Note that a pause at the end of a line is not a caesura.

Chiasmus: Chiasmus consists of two parallel phrases in which corresponding words or phrases are placed in the opposite order: "Fair is foul, foul is fair."

Cliché: Clichés are phrases or expressions that are used so much in everyday life, that people roll their eyes when they hear them. For example, "dead as a doornail" is a cliché. In good poetry, clichés are never used with a straight face, so if you see one, consider why the speaker might be using it.

Concrete Poetry: Concrete poetry conveys meaning by how it looks on the page. It's not a super-accurate term, and it can refer to a lot of different kinds of poems. One classic example is poems that look like they thing they describe. The French poet Guillaume Apollinaire wrote a poem about Paris in the shape of the Eiffel tower.

Connotation: The suggestive meaning of a word – the associations it brings up. The reason

it's not polite to call a mentally-handicapped person "retarded" is that the word has a *negative* connotation. Connotations depend a lot on the culture and experience of the person reading the word. For some people, the word "liberal" has a positive connotation. For others, it's negative. Think of connotation as the murky haze hanging around the literal meaning of a word. Trying to figure out connotations of words can be one of the most confusing and fascinating aspects of reading poetry.

Contradiction: Two statements that don't seem to agree with each other. "I get sober when I drink alcohol" is a contradiction. Some contradictions, like "paradox" (see our definition below), are only apparent, and they become true when you think about them in a certain way.

Denotation: The literal, straightforward meaning of a word. It's "dictionary definition." The word "cat" denotes an animal with four legs and a habit of coughing up furballs.

Dramatic Monologue: You can think of a dramatic monologue in poetry as a speech taken from a play that was never written. Okay, maybe that's confusing. It's a poem written in the voice of a fictional character and delivered to a fictional listener, instead of in the voice of a poet to his or her readers. The British poet Robert Browning is one of the most famous writers of dramatic monologues. They are "dramatic" because they can be acted out, just like a play, and they are monologues because they consist of just one person speaking to another person, just as a "dialogue" consists of two people speaking. (The prefix "mono" means "one," whereas "di" means "two").

Elegy: An elegy is a poem about a dead person or thing. Whenever you see a poem with the title, "In Memory of . . .", for example, you're talking about an elegy. Kind of like that two-line poem you wrote for your pet rabbit Bubbles when you were five years old. Poor, poor Bubbles.

Ellipsis: You see ellipses all the time, usually in the form of "…". An ellipsis involves leaving out or suppressing words. It's like . . . well, you get the idea.

Enjambment: When a phrase carries over a line-break without a major pause. In French, the word means, "straddling," which we think is a perfect way to envision an enjambed line. Here's an example of enjambment from a poem by Joyce Kilmer: 'I think that I shall never see / A poem as lovely as a tree." The sentence continues right over the break with only a slight pause.

Extended metaphor: A central metaphor that acts like an "umbrella" to connect other metaphors or comparisons within it. It can span several lines or an entire poem. When one of Shakespeare's characters delivers an entire speech about how all the world is a stage and people are just actors, that's extended metaphor, with the idea of "theater" being the umbrella connecting everything.

Foot: The most basic unit of a poem's meter, a foot is a combination of long and short syllables. There are all kinds of different feet, such as "LONG-short" and "short-short-LONG." The first three words of the famous holiday poem, "'Twas the Night before Christmas," are one metrical foot (short-short-LONG). By far the most important foot to know is the iamb: short-LONG. An iamb is like one heartbeat: ba-DUM.

Free Verse: "Free bird! Play free bird!" Oops, we meant "Free verse! Define free verse!" Free verse is a poetic style that lacks a regular meter or rhyme scheme. This may sound like free verse has no style at all, but usually there is some recognizable consistency to the writer's use of rhythm. Walt Whitman was one of the pioneers of free verse, and nobody ever had trouble identifying a Whitman poem.

Haiku: A poetic form invented by the Japanese. In English, the haiku has three sections with five syllables, seven syllables, and five syllables respectively. They often describe natural imagery and include a word that reveals the season in which the poem is set. Aside from its three sections, the haiku also traditionally features a sharp contrast between two ideas or images.

Heroic Couplet: Heroic couplets are rhyming pairs of verse in iambic pentameter. What on earth did this "couplets" do to become "heroic"? Did they pull a cat out of a tree or save an old lady from a burning building? In fact, no. They are called "heroic" because in the old days of English poetry they were used to talk about the trials and adventures of heroes. Although heroic couplets totally ruled the poetry scene for a long time, especially in the 17th and 18th centuries, nowadays they can sound kind of old-fashioned.

Hyperbole: A hyperbole is a gross exaggeration. For example, "tons of money" is a hyperbole.

Iambic Pentameter: Here it is, folks. Probably the single most useful technical term in poetry. Let's break it down: an "iamb" is an unaccented syllable followed by an accented one. "Penta" means "five," and "meter" refers to a regular rhythmic pattern. So "iambic pentameter" is a kind of *rhythmic pattern* that consist of *five iambs* per line. It's the most common rhythm in English poetry and sounds like five heartbeats: ba-DUM, ba-DUM, ba-DUM, ba-DUM, ba-DUM. Let's try it out on the first line of Shakespeare's *Romeo and Juliet*: "In fair Verona, where we lay our scene." Every second syllable is accented, so this is classic iambic pentameter.

Imagery: Imagery is intense, descriptive language in a poem that helps to trigger our senses and our memories when we read it.

Irony: Irony involves saying one thing while really meaning another, contradictory thing.

Metaphor: A metaphor happens when one thing is described as being another thing. "You're a toad!" is a metaphor – although not a very nice one. And metaphor is different from simile because it leaves out the words "like" or "as." For example, a simile would be, "You're *like* a toad."

Metonymy: Metonymy happens when some attribute of what is being described is used to indicate some other attribute. When talking about the power of a king, for example, one may instead say "the crown"-- that is, the physical attribute that is usually identified with royalty and power.

Ode: A poem written in praise or celebration of a person, thing, or event. Odes have been

written about everything from famous battles and lofty emotions to family pets and household appliances. What would you write an ode about?

Onomatopoeia: Besides being a really fun word to say aloud, onomatopoeia refers either to words that resemble in sound what they represent. For example, do you hear the hissing noise when you say the word "hiss" aloud? And the old Batman television show *loved* onomatopoeia: "Bam! Pow! Kaplow!"

Oxymoron: An oxymoron is the combination of two terms ordinarily seen as opposites. For example, "terribly good" is an oxymoron.

Paradox: A statement that contradicts itself and nonetheless seems true. It's a paradox when John Donne writes, "Death, thou shalt die," because he's using "death" in two different senses. A more everyday example might be, "Nobody goes to the restaurant because it's too crowded."

Parallelism: Parallelism happens a lot in poetry. It is the similarity of structure in a pair or series of related words, phrases, or clauses. Julius Caesar's famous words, "I came, I saw, I conquered," are an example of parallelism. Each clause begins with "I" and ends with a verb.

Pastoral: A poem about nature or simple, country life. If the poem you're reading features babbling brooks, gently swaying trees, hidden valleys, rustic haystacks, and sweetly singing maidens, you're probably dealing with a pastoral. The oldest English pastoral poems were written about the English countryside, but there are plenty of pastorals about the American landscape, too.

Personification: Personification involves giving human traits (qualities, feelings, action, or characteristics) to non-living objects (things, colors, qualities, or ideas).

Pun: A pun is a play on words. Puns show us the multiple meanings of a word by replacing that word with another that is similar in sound but has a very different meaning. For example, "when Shmoop went trick-or-treating in a Batman costume, he got lots of snickers." Hehe.

Quatrain: A stanza with four lines. Quatrains are the most common stanza form.

Refrain: A refrain is a regularly recurring phrase or verse especially at the end of each stanza or division of a poem or song. For example in T.S. Eliot's *Love Song for J. Alfred Prufrock*, the line, "in the room the women come and go / Talking of Michelangelo" is a refrain.

Rhetorical Question: Rhetorical questions involve asking a question for a purpose other than obtaining the information requested. For example, when we ask, "Shmoop, are you nuts?", we are mainly expressing our belief that Shmoop is crazy. In this case, we don't really expect Shmoop to tell us whether or not they are nuts.

Rhyming Couplet: A rhyming couplet is a pair of verses that rhyme. It's the simplest and most common rhyme scheme, but it can have more complicated variations (see "Heroic Couplet" for one example).

Simile: Similes compare one thing directly to another. For example, "My love is like a burning flame" is a simile. You can quickly identify similes when you see the words "like" or "as" used, as in "x is like y." Similes are different from metaphors – for example, a metaphor would refer to "the burning flame of my love."

Slam: A form of contemporary poetry that is meant to be performed at informal competitions rather than read. Slam readings are often very political in nature and draw heavily from the rhythms and energy of hip-hop music.

Slant Rhyme: A rhyme that isn't quite a rhyme. The words "dear" and "door" form a slant rhyme. The words sound similar, but they aren't close enough to make a full rhyme.

Sonnet: A well-known poetic form. Two of the most famous examples are the sonnets of William Shakespeare and John Donne. A traditional sonnet has fourteen lines in iambic pentameter and a regular rhyme scheme. Sonnets also feature a "turn" somewhere in the middle, where the poem takes a new direction or changes its argument in some way. This change can be subtle or really obvious. Although we English-speaking folks would love to take credit fort this amazing form, it was actually developed by the Italians and didn't arrive in England until the 16th century.

Speaker: The speaker is the voice *behind* the poem – the person we imagine to be speaking. It's important to note that the speaker is *not* the poet. Even if the poem is biographical, you should treat the speaker as a fictional creation, because the writer is choosing what to say about himself. Besides, even poets don't speak in poetry in their everyday lives – although it would be cool if they did.

Stanza: A division within a poem where a group of lines are formed into a unit. The word "stanza" comes from the Italian word for "room." Just like a room, a poetic stanza is set apart on a page by four "walls" of blank, white space.

Symbol: Generally speaking, a symbol is a sign representing something other than itself.

Synecdoche: In synecdoche a part of something represents the whole. For example: "One does not live by bread alone." The statement assumes that bread is representative of all categories of food.

Syntax: In technical terms, syntax is the study of how to put sentences together. In poetry, "syntax" refers to the way words and phrases relate to each other. Some poems have a syntax similar to everyday prose of spoken English (like the sentences you're reading right now). Other poems have a crazier syntax, where it's hard to see how things fit together at all. It can refer to the order of words in a sentence, like Yoda's wild syntax from the *Star Wars* movies: "A very important concept in poetry, syntax is!" Or, more figuratively, it can refer to the organization of ideas or topics in a poem: "Why did the poet go from talking about his mother to a description of an ostrich?"

Understatement: An understatement seeks to express a thought or impression by

underemphasizing the extent to which a statement may be true. Understatement is the opposite of hyperbole and is frequently used for its comedic value in articles, speeches, etc. when issues of great importance are being discussed. Ex: "There's just one, tiny, little problem with that plan – it'll get us all killed!"

Sources:

http://allpoetry.com/column/2339540
http://academic.reed.edu/writing/paper_help/figurative_language.html
http://web.uvic.ca/wguide/Pages/LiteraryTermsTOC.html#RhetLang
http://www.tnellen.com/cybereng/lit_terms/allegory.html

Printed in Great Britain
by Amazon.co.uk, Ltd.,
Marston Gate.